THE REPRESENTATIONS OF ARABS AND MUSLIMS IN U.S. WAR CINEMA

By:

Noor Mubarak Bajuwaiber

ACKNOWLEDGMENTS

Since my arrival in Australia in February 2010, I started my Masters course in Communication Studies in the Faculty of Arts at The University of Western Australia. The last two years have passed very quickly and I really have enjoyed every moment of the time with my small little young man, my son and with my studies.

After one year and a half of Masters study, it is finally time to finish my dissertation and have a chance to acknowledge the people who have helped me in all kind of ways. Apart from the efforts of myself, the success of my dissertation depends largely first on my faith in god.

Finally, I have the opportunity to express my sincere and deepest gratitude and thanks to Dr. Stewart Woods my supervisor, who was absolutely helpful, patient and offered invaluable assistance, support, guidance and inspiration. Thank you very much for your support and I will never forget your great ideas you offered me, and how you helped me a lot to solve the problems together. By this acknowledgment, I would show you my greatest appreciation and thank you is not enough for your tremendous support and help.

Mohammed Fares, thank you very much for editing and correcting the grammar of my dissertation. It was such a great help from you.

Areej Aseeri, I would like to thank you for giving me the opportunity to deal with a great editor who helped a lot by proof reading my dissertation.

My brother Mohammed, thank you very much for giving me the chance to understand the wars in very simple way. How can I express my thanks to you? Without your simplicity in explaining the wars, I couldn't understand them.

My family, Mom and Dad, Thank you a lot for your care.

My Son Hamad, Thank you my little young man, you are the most beautiful thing I have ever seen in the world. Your smile every morning giving me the energy to finish this dissertation. I love you so much.

DEDICATION

I dedicate this dissertation to my love, my husband who supported me each step of all the way and for his support, patience, understanding and encouragement.

ABSTRACT

This dissertation examines the way Arabs are stereotyped in Hollywood war films. The dissertation shows how the enemy is portrayed in Hollywood war films. After World War II Nazis were the enemy in Hollywood combat films, and most of the films about WWII, depict Nazis as such. After WWII, the role of the enemy shifted from the Nazis to the Vietnamese. The fear of communism and the victory after the Cold War led Hollywood to depict Vietnamese as enemy in Vietnam War combat films. To study the way the Arabs are stereotyped in Hollywood war films, this dissertation makes a comparison between the depiction of these historical enemies and the representation of Iraqis in war films. By analysing motion pictures produced by Hollywood following each war, similarities and differences are identified in the way enemies are portrayed.

TABLE OF CONTENTS

Introduction

Mass media serves a number of functions in society today including the communication of social heritage and the transmission of philosophical cultural and social values which maintain the society. As a primary channel of communication mass media is utilised to disseminate information to a large, diverse audience. It is also the most accessible source of news and information. Through its delivery of information, mass media tends to influence public opinion and the decisions that people make. One type of mass media are films, or movies, which encompass motion pictures that are produced by various film production companies. As one of the most important art forms today, films aim to entertain, inspire, and teach. More importantly, they impact their audience. Accordingly, films influence the shaping and reshaping of the culture of a society.

This influence on society is evident through movies produced in Hollywood, one of the largest producers of various types and genres of movies, including those that depict what happened in some of the world's historical wars. War movies rarely fail to attract the attention of many moviegoers. Amongst the most common topics in Hollywood is the depiction of World War II, the Vietnam War and the Iraq War. In creating films about real conflicts, Hollywood is required to portray the enemy of the Americans at that time, which were the Nazis, the Vietnamese and the Arabs. This dissertation aims to analyse and evaluate the representation of Iraqis in Hollywood war movies, analysing how the Iraqis are portrayed in comparison to the Nazis and Vietnamese.

The Making of Hollywood War Movies

The studio years of the late 1920s to the early 1960s were regarded as the golden era of the film industry, wherein movies were the main source of information and entertainment. The success of the studio years eventually waned upon the inception of television, where entertainment became confined in the home. Although the success of the studio years has diminished and the number of moviegoers has declined considerably, the movie industry has remained an essential part of the American culture.

Media is gradually becoming a most powerful force of society. It aims to inform, entertain and sometimes persuade the general public. However, some of the messages, information and images reflected in the media are partisan. Furthermore, media is an entity that can be manipulated by people; thus the objectivity lies in the hands of the perpetrators behind the various media. The images and messages that are shown by media depend on the perceptions, beliefs and values of the people producing the content of a particular media. However, James Watson argues in his book *Media Communication: an Introduction to Theory and Process* that media are capable of activating audiences and deactivating them, as well as the fewer the various sources of information there are in the world of media, the more likely the media will affect the audience thoughts, behaviours and attitudes (1998). He also mentions that due to the society changes and conflicts, the media could increase a high degree of structural instability and security (1998, p. 65). In an information society like ours, media is becoming extremely critical since the messages are conveyed in various forms through digital and electronic transmission.

Stereotypical Representations

Stereotyping is defined as a popular belief or knowledge about specific people that can cause damage to the concept of self. Brunsch describes a stereotype as 'a fixed idea or image people have a particular type of person or thing but which is not always true in reality.' (2005, p. 3) Increasing awareness about this issue, particularly the damage stereotyping can render, has led to an attempt to eradicate the prevalence of this particular trend in media (McConnell, 2003). Currently, there is an overwhelming influx of images that have a negative impact on people viewing these images. In fact, these images create a reflection of society that does not align with the reality (McConnell, 2002). Despite all of the negative effects of stereotyping in the media, it is unavoidable. Stereotyping occurs frequently in advertising and other types of media that require easy understanding of messages. The use of stereotypes is typically derived from the identification of a group:

Stereotype formation begins when an aggregate of persons is perceived as comprising a group, an entity. When a set of persons is perceived to be a group, it is likely that the group is also distinguished from other groups. Thus, individuals are categorized into different groups that are somehow perceived in relation to each other (Women vs. Men; Democrats vs. Republicans; Poles vs. Italians vs. Germans). (Macrae *et. al.,* 1996, p. 44)

Stereotyping proliferated by media can cause problems since it reduces the diversity of people in categories. The unreal characteristics of a particular group are transformed into reality. In addition, stereotypes are used to justify those in the position or in possession of power. It also propagates the idea of discrimination and disparity. As Lawrence H. Suid notes, there are no limits to stereotyping in Hollywood combat films, and the characterizations of the enemy in movies made during war became more sharply described (2002, p. 71).

Literature Review

Arabs are frequently portrayed in a variety of American mass media and there are numerous books and writers that discuss the representation of Arabs in the media. A former news consultant on Middle East affairs and Professor Jack M. Shaheen argues in his article *Media Coverage of the Middle East: Perception and Foreign Policy* that Arabs are stereotyped in American popular culture noting that the American media portray Arabs with 'rigid, repetitive and repulsive depictions that demonize and delegitimize the Arab' (1997). In the book *The U.S. Media and the Middle East: Image and Perception*, Mahboub Hashim examines coverage of the portrayal of Arabs between 1990 and 1993 in two leading U.S. news magazines, *Time* and *Newsweek*. Hashim finds that coverage of Arabs was mostly negative, especially in the years 1990 and 1991 (1995, p. 154). He also states that media reports of Arabs are mostly about attacks, invasions, killings and kidnappings, and that positive content is lower than negative content.

In the article *Arabs and the Media*, Narmeen El-Farra examines the way Arabs are portrayed in media and notes that:

> The Western media has often projected individuals of Arabs descent in a negative manner. Currently, Arabs are seen as terrorists and murderers due to how the media represents them. Newspapers use key words such as extremists, terrorists, fanatics to describe Arabs. (1996)

Shaheen also conducted research into the way Arabs and Muslims are portrayed on television and writes that:

> The popular caricature of the average Arab is as mythical as the old portrait of Jew: He is robed and turbaned, sinister and dangerous, engaged mainly in hijacking airlines and blowing up public buildings. (1997).

Shaheen also examines the portrayal of Arabs and Muslims as the enemy in Hollywood war films in his article *Hollywood's Muslim Arab*, and he notes that:

> The Arab people have always had the roughest and most comprehending deal from Hollywood, but with the death of Cold War, the stereotype has been granted even more prominence. (2000)

Many writers, authors and critics agree that Arabs are mostly portrayed in a negative way with an absence of positive representation. Moreover, the image of Arabs in American media and Hollywood war films has not changed significantly for decades (Vandermey, *et. at.,* 2009).

More specifically related to this research, a number of books and texts discuss the portrayal of the enemy in war films. Clayton R. Koppes and Gregory D. Black undertook an extensive study of the way Hollywood depicts the enemy in war films. They write that 'if America and its allies were the epitome of righteousness, the enemy embodied all evil' (1987, p. 248). Koppes and Black also examine the nature of propaganda regarding the enemy in Hollywood films. During World War II war films, the Nazis and the Japanese were the enemy and during the Cold War and Vietnam War films, Communists including Koreans, Vietnamese and Russians are the enemy. Yet, after the fall of communism, Arabs become the alternative enemy in Hollywood war films (1990).

In the following chapter I will examine the representation of the Nazis and the Vietnamese in American war films. In chapter three I will then compare this with Hollywood's representation of Iraqis.

Chapter One

The Representation of Nazis in American War Films

During the period between the 1930s and 1940s, Hollywood maintained a significant authority in cinema. Films that were produced in Hollywood's most influential and dominant studios were filled with the biggest and most famous stars. In 1941, Hollywood studios began portraying the National Socialist ideology of "Nazism" in a major way, following the involvement of the United States in World War II after the attack on Pearl Harbour. Before 1941 and prior to the involvement of the United States in WWII, although there were some movies portraying the Nazis, producers in Hollywood were hesitant to depict the rise of the Nazis in their films despite the attention that the movement had created. Hollywood was unenthusiastic to produce films about Nazis due to the fear of Nazism, as well as for fear that Hollywood would lose its domination, universality and authority. Hitler announced an official boycott of Jewish business in April 1933 and then two months later limited distribution of Hollywood films (Ross, 2004). Another reason was that Hollywood studios during the period of uprising Nazism was dominated by Jews who were frightened and doubtful about depicting Nazis in movies.

> Most studios, even those led by Jews, were hesitant to criticize the German regime, reflecting their sensitivity that such scripts would call attention on their Jewish origins, problematic in an era of increasing anti-Semitism in both Europe and America where isolationism was popular. (Biskupski, 2010)

In spite of this, Hollywood produced numerous films about WWII, and the depiction of Nazis differ from films that were produced before the attack on Pearl Harbour on 1941 and after it. Nazis were portrayed before and after WWII as evil leaders, brutes, heartless, untrustworthy, bloodthirsty and obedient. However, movies after WWII focus more on the human personality ideas and themes about the nature of war in which the representation of Nazis as enemies diverged between the period before the 1940s and the period between the 1950s and 1970s.

In the book *We'll always have the movies: American Ccinema During World War II*, Robert L. McLaughlin and Sally E. Parry discuss the way the Nazis were depicted in Hollywood movies, noting that Nazis leaders were presented in Hollywood films as unstable, perverse, wicked and hypocritical (2006, p. 104). Films produced by Hollywood give a variety of Nazi stereotypes. In one movie, Nazis are depicted as cultured people, where in another Nazis were depicted as sadists who enjoy killing, for example, *Where Eagles Dare* (1968), *The Dirty Dozen* (1967), *The Great Escape* (1963), *Confession of a Nazi Spy* (1939) *and The Great Dictator* (1940). However, in many Hollywood movies about WWII mostly the common quote that the viewer can find the Nazis soldiers say is " I'm just a soldier doing my job", they were represented as mindless people who are just obeying the rules of the leader. As Frank Manchel argues:

> During the war years, Hollywood set its patterns on how Germans should be treated. They were to be stereotyped on two levels; either as brutes, in the form of the Gestapo, SS troops and hired henchmen, or as German intellectuals trapped by their inability to deviate from a preconceived idea. (1990, p. 263)

The theme of Nazis as brutes can be seen in the anti-Nazi film *Confessions of a Nazi Spy* directed by Anatole Litvak. The story of this movie is about an FBI agent, Ed Renard played by Edward Robinson, who had been effective in detecting a Nazi spy in the United States before the war. *Confessions of a Nazi Spy* caused controversy due to movie scenes that showed Germans as evil people. One example is Francis Lederer who played the role as Kurt Schneider, a former U.S. soldier who works as a spy for the German Intelligence. His evil character is revealed when he confesses to Renard about the intercepting communication from Nazis operating in U.K. that he learned about (Booker, 1999). Michael E. Birdwell argues in his book *Celluloid Soldiers: The Warner Bros. Campaign Against Nazism* that:

> [Jack] Warner boasted to them [members of the Nazi high echelon] that the studio was currently preparing a picture called Confessions of a Nazi Spy, which would hurt the Nazi elite far more than a political assassination. (Birdwell, 1999, p. 57)

The theme of Nazis as brutes is illustrated in a comedic way in the film *The Great Dictator*. The story of this comedy film is based on the rise of Hitler, Nazism, Fascism and anti-Semitism. Charlie Chaplin, lead actor, director, writer and producer started filming this movie one week after Hitler attacked Poland in World War II. Charlie Chaplin played the character of Hitler in a comical way, which provoked Hitler's anger. Indeed, as Dan Kamin notes that, 'Hitler put Chaplin at risk personally; he received death threats and crank letters throughout the preparation of the film.' (2008, p. 154)

The Great Escape is another film that depicts Nazis as brutes as well as German intellectuals, both of whom are just obeying orders. *The Great Escape* is a film that is based on a true story of escaped allied prisoners of war (POW) from Stalag Luft III German Camp during WWII. The film represents the story of POWs who plan an escape from the high security camp, and the challenges they face in the camp. The film also shows the procedure of digging a tunnel to escape. However, the latter portion focuses on the escapees after the escape as most of them have been recaptured. The representation of German Nazis in this film can be connected with the two themes, the brute Nazis and the intellectual Germans. As Ian Roberts points out, '*The Great Escape* (1963) established a stereotype of the faceless German infantryman led by brutal, ideologically suspect Nazi.' (Haines *et al*, 2010, p. 82)

The first brute Nazis were stereotyped in *The Great Escape*; however, this film did not dehumanise the Nazis, but rather pictured them as intellectual people who have skills and obey orders. This was portrayed in the way they recaptured or killed most of the escapees, as Captain Virgil Hilts played by Steve McQueen, and Flight Lieutenant Bob Hendley played by James Garner. Yet, the Nazis were also portrayed as brutes in the scene when the black-leather-coated Gestapo agent orders the murder of 50 escapees. This scene shows how the Nazis are bloodthirsty, where killing others is the best solution to solve problems.

Intellectual Nazis were depicted again in *Where Eagles Dare*. In the book *Performing Difference: Representations of "The Other" in Film and Theater*, Thomas Christopher discusses *Where Eagles Dare* as causing confusion where the viewer does not know 'who is on whose side' (2009). This film is an example of putting the viewer in a dilemma of knowing who is the enemy and who is the friend.

> For three quarters of the movie the viewer is led to believe that British Special Forces are on a mission to rescue a captured American General. In actuality, the mission is designed to flush out a horde of German spies that have infiltrated British Intelligence. (Friedman, 2009, p. 253)

In post-WWII movies like *Where Eagles Dare* and *The Great Escape*, the audience can distinguish between the "good" Germans who defended and fought for their country, and the "bad' Germans who are the evil Nazis portrayed as mechanistic servants. Moreover, in *Where Eagles Dare* the plot of the movie is to rescue an American General who was captured by the Germans before the Nazis interrogate him. The movie portrayed the Nazis as people who are only following orders under the rule of Hitler. This portrayal illustrates the theme of depicting Nazis as people who have skills, yet at the same time senselessly and mindlessly follow the rules. In the climactic scene of the film, the main Nazi characters, "the Gestapo" officers, are sitting around a conference table to interrogate the American General George Carnaby, played by Robert Beatty. The image of Nazis in this scene is that of cultured people who wear uniforms and follow the rules. The Nazi officer picks up the phone and points to a female officer to do her job. The female officer then opens her purse to begin torturing the American officer.

> Crude as this stereotype was in the context of World War II filmmaking, it nevertheless provided a sort of cultural-political analysis of Nazi behavior, rooted in a "national character" that allowed the same characteristics to explain both the evils of Nazism and the willingness of its subject to obey." (Gianos, 1998, p. 119)

Hollywood portrayal of Nazis has particular characteristics. These characteristics can be found in Hollywood movies either before the war or after the war. One of these characteristics is portraying the Nazis as evil and cruel. Another characteristic that can be found in Hollywood movies, and is obvious in the above two movies, is increased focus on uniforms and following orders.

The Representation of the Vietnamese in American War Films

The importance of the Vietnam War led Hollywood to produce many war movies about that era. Vietnam War films represented various stories about either the Americans or the Vietnamese. Some of these films portrayed American soldiers and how they were affected by the war, while other films criticised the American involvement in the Vietnam War. Since the end of the Vietnam War in 1975, many films have represented the conflict of this war by presenting military characters, elements of the anti-war American movement, or other war-related stories. Hollywood movie productions about the Vietnam War have focused on the representation of the enemy who are the Vietnamese, and/or American veterans of the war.

> Hollywood produced a series of films that glorified the war in Vietnam. They have on the whole been permeated the macho-warrior and racist ideology, reaffirming a neo-Cold War perspective of the world and depicting radical and liberal-minded people as weak and deviant. (Dittmar and Michaud, 2000, p. 20)

However, there was less portrayal of the Vietnamese in these films, stressing that these representations expose more about the American history than the Vietnamese themselves. As the Vietnamese were depicted in many Hollywood films, many themes could be seen in the portrayal of the enemy. However, the Vietnamese in films were most often portrayed as animals, uncultured barbarians who shot to wound not to kill.

In this section, I will focus on two major themes in the representation of Vietnamese in Hollywood movies. However, the first theme I will focus on is the dehumanised enemy, in other words, the way the Vietnamese were depicted in Hollywood films as animals and barbarians. For example, the theme of dehumanising the Vietnamese enemy in *The Deer Hunter* (1978) was portrayed when the film relocated to Vietnam. This film is about three friends, Michael played by Robert De Niro, Steve played by John Savage and Nick played by Christopher Walken, who go deer hunting. Upon their return to plan their friend's wedding, they were sent by the U.S. army to serve in Vietnam. The movie then continues to give the story about how these three men were affected by the war after the Vietcong captured them in North Vietnam. The dehumanised enemy is revealed in the Russian Roulette scene as well as other scenes. The Russian Roulette scene represented the Vietnamese as barbarians, merciless and sadistic who killed innocent victims. They shot not to kill but to damage and wound. When the three friends were captured as prisoners, the guards forced them to hurt each other. In their book, *Diversity in U.S. Mass Media*, Catherine Luther et. al., analysed the representation of Vietnamese in *The Deer Hunter* in a very specific way.

> In the film's [*The Deer Hunter*] other scenes too, the North Vietnamese are portrayed as animalistic. For example, a North Vietnamese soldier is shown in one scene killing Vietnamese civilians, including women and young children. (Luther *et al*, 2011, p. 13)

Many critics wrote about *The Deer Hunter* and the dehumanised representation of the Vietnamese. Ray Browne and Pat Browne, in their book *The Guide to United States Popular Culture* analyse some of the Vietnam War movies including *The Deer Hunter*. They discuss categories of Vietnam films. The first category they mention is films that 'portrayed Vietnam veterans as tightly wound, antisocial loners about to go over the edge.' (2001, p. 879)

> *The Deer Hunter* is an important and controversial film for two reasons...it was the first major Hollywood production since the *Green Berets* to feature the Vietnamese, especially the North Vietnamese and Vietcong, as brutal and inhuman people. This characterization outraged many liberal viewers, leading charges that *The Deer Hunter* is a racist film. (2001, p. 879)

It is well known that most of the war film genres are about dehumanising the other side, the "enemy". As in the book *Franklin D. Roosevelt and Shaping of American Political Culture*, the writer points out that:

> The film industry worked closely with the office of War Information, producing films to explain the war effort to the American people and providing feature films...which instituted a formula based on dehumanizing the enemy and celebrating the melting pot concept of American society. (Briley, 2001, p. 30)

The second key theme in the Vietnam War films is the theme of de-individuated enemy. The Vietnamese were often depicted with no individuality or characters, they were represented with the same characteristics, they look the same and they sound the same. A good example of this is *Apocalypse Now* (1979). This Film is about Willard, played by Martin Sheen, an American soldier who has flashbacks about the Vietnam War. Although the movie is about the Vietnam War, it did not address the conflict between the enemy soldiers, the Vietnamese and the American soldiers; rather, the plot of the movie focused more on the conflict within the American soldier. The theme of neglecting the identity of the Vietnamese is evident through the reduced number of scenes of Vietnamese in the film. The enemy in *Apocalypse Now* have no names or specific characters. As M. Keith Booker states in his book, *From Box Office to Ballot Box: The American Political Film*, according to idea in which the movie neglected the Vietnamese '…treating the enemy forces as simply another in a series of natural obstacles (heat, rain, disease, insects, snakes) that are announced by the American forces in the jungles of Vietnam' (2007, p. 167).

Apocalypse Now is based on the novel *The Heart of Darkness* written by Joseph Conrad. The theme of neglecting the identity of the enemy is the major similarity between the novel and the movie. On one hand, the movie shows the minimal presence of the Vietnamese; for example, in one of the movie dialogues, Willard is told that he is fighting the biggest nothing in east "Vietnam." In other words, Vietnamese are nothing. On the other hand, the novel neglects Africans whose country the British colonised. The entire story is about imperialism and the power of Great Britain. Goonetilleke makes a comparison between the novel and the movie, by saying that in Joseph Conrad's *Heart of Darkness* 'Marlow subscribes to a code of conduct…whereas Willard, a hired assassin, does not subscribe to any such codes and does/says nothing to contradict the references to Vietnamese as "savages".' (2007, p. 134)

The theme of the de-individuated enemy can be seen as well in *The Deer Hunter* and *Platoon* (1986). Furthermore, the de-individuated enemy in *The Deer Hunter* film is portrayed as people who look alike, sound the same, and have similar characteristics. In the scene when the three friends were prisoners by the

North Vietnamese, the Vietnamese men were represented as "yellow peril" (Luther *et al,* 2011). The theme of the de-individuated enemy is also evident in the Russian Roulette scene, in which all the Vietnamese in the scene look alike and are presented as savages. Moreover, there are no Vietnamese characters as none of the Vietnamese had a speaking role.

The themes of the dehumanised and de-individuated enemy can be exemplified in the movie *Platoon.* This is not to say that *The Deer Hunter* and *Apocalypse Now* do not have the two themes; however, *Platoon* has the most evident combination of the de-individuated and dehumanised enemy. *Platoon* was written and directed by Oliver Stone. Stone served in Vietnam as an infantryman, and he wrote this film based on his tragic experiences in Vietnam. He portrayed the war from his perspective as he was living the war during the period he served in Vietnam. 'Oliver Stone wrote *Platoon* from the first-hand-recollection of a combat infantryman.' (Rubin, 2011, p. 184) In the film, the role of Chris Taylor played by Charlie Sheen is Stone representing himself where he served in the war. The film is about Chris, a veteran who served in Vietnam and observed/witnessed a conflict between the good person Sergeant Elias, played by Willem Dafoe, and the bad person Sergeant Barnes, played by Tom Berenger in the American troops. The story continues with battles until the end when Chris kills Barnes in revenge because Barnes guns down Elias to death.

On the one hand, the de-individuated enemy can be seen in almost the entire movie, beginning with the voiceover of the director and ending with the shooting of Barnes. In *Platoon,* there were no scenes in which the viewer can see battles between the Americans and the Vietnamese. The enemy in *Platoon* is faceless and nameless, people who are hiding in the jungles and wearing red headbands that the American soldiers can barely catch and shoot. On the other hand, the dehumanisation of the Vietnamese is evident in *Platoon* as this movie portrayed the Vietnamese as savages and barbarians. Maureen Ryan discusses the Vietnam War in his book saying that ''Oliver Stones' *Platoon*...stereotypes about the Vietnamese as small, sneaky "gooks who are alien, mysterious and distinctly "other".' (2008, p. 254)

Conclusion

An important facet of human culture and experience is war. Through images and words in films and movies, history can be brought to life for audiences because movies are an influential and powerful cultural device. In concluding this chapter, I will examine the impact of Hollywood WWII and Vietnam War films on the American society and culture.

> Films have the ability to evoke the mood and tone of a society in a particular era…by films, one means not merely documentaries, which obviously directly capture something of the reality of people's lives and feelings, but also mainstream *Hollywood* commercial films…that confront American society. (Auster and Quart, 2011)

The narrative of war films can shape the public opinion towards any case or the viewpoint of the filmmaker. Furthermore, in the case of films dealing with WWII and Vietnam War the storylines in those movies could narrate many different perspectives and viewpoints from the filmmakers regarding the war. For example, WWII or Vietnam War films can tell the audience a story from the a viewpoint of prisoners who want to escape as in *The Great Escape* or from the perspective of an active soldier as in *Apocalypse Now*. I will focus on the interactions of American society regarding the war films and cultural changes due to the motion pictures of WWII and Vietnam War. Philip L. Gianos mentions in his book *Politics and Politicians in American Film*, the audience of the WWII film and writes that:

> The approach of the Second World War [Films] was watched closely by the U.S. film industry, many in that industry were refugees from Nazi Germany, and the industry watched the coming war closely because it was concerned about the loss of Europeans markets. (1998, p. 105)

The movies that were produced about WWII and the Vietnam War were not made by Hollywood to only entertain the audience, but also to enhance nationalism and patriotism in the Americans viewers. Moreover, in the book *Ground, Warfare: an International Encyclopedia,* Jari Eloranta states that 'Movies and films have influenced how society views and thinks about warfare.' (2002, p. 274) In addition, Eloranta notes that films about war could impart cultural values and dispositions as well as providing propaganda for national causes (2002).

On one hand, WWII movies made before the involvement of the United States in 1941, for example, *Confession of a Nazi Spy* and *The Great Dictator*, helped to motivate the spirits of patriotism in the American audience, though these movies provided messages, as justification is important and necessary to avoid the destruction of the Nazis and to support the defeat of the enemy.

> Charlie Chaplin portrayed a buffoonish Adolf Hitler-like character in *The Great Dictator* (1940). Yet not only was Hollywood trying to alarm the nation to outside threats, but it had rallied around the Roosevelt administration and produced patriotic films. (2002, p. 275)

Furthermore, films post-WWII reflect to the American audience their society and history as *Where Eagles Dare*. Thus, to explain the above idea, Michael Klein points out that films about WWII focused on a wounded, alienated, or rejected veteran's return to the American society and he continues his argument and writes that 'such films were often vehicles for social criticism and thus were a recognisable popular culture form.' (Dittmar and Michaud, 2000, p. 21) Generally, movies about WWII, whether before the U.S. involvement or after, were the vehicle for assisting the Americans to know about the war and understand it. Hollywood films about WWII asked the viewers to think about the implication of Nazis. This means that Hollywood films have a tremendous impact on the American culture and society.

> Hollywood films, because they were seen by huge numbers of people over the whole country [United States], were the most efficient and powerful means of communicating ideas about American national identity and America's enemies in the 1940s. (McLaughlin and Parry, 2006, p. 100)

On the other hand, one of the most problematical wars in the American history is Vietnam War. Due to this fact, Hollywood filmmakers produced a lot of movies about Vietnam War. 'The Vietnam War is the second most traumatic, contentious, and problematic event in the U.S. history—the first being the Civil War.' (Solheim, 2008, p. 4) However, Vietnam War films captured the American audiences especially the sentiment of people who were against the War. Klein argues that:

> Vietnam as a subject initially returned to the Hollywood screen after conclusion of the war in the form of a series of coming home films that focused on the situation of the returning veteran. (Dittmar and Michaud, 2000, p. 21)

The movies about Vietnam War created an emotional significance through the dramatic depiction of the cruelty of the phenomenon and the shock that ruined the American soldiers who were enlisted and conscripted. Yet, it was not only the American soldiers in Vietnam movies that captured the audiences' emotions, but the portrayal of the Vietnamese as well, and the way they were dehumanised. Vietnam War films were focused more on the psychology and the experiences of the American soldier than on the Vietnamese. According to Vietnam War combat films audience, Bran J. Woodman points out that:

> These films [Vietnam War Combat films] often attempted to reveal to U.S. audiences the "authentic" war experiences of the American soldier in Vietnam, or the way Vietnam "really was' for American soldiers fighting there. (2005, p. 90)

Technically, many critics pointed to the depiction of the Vietnam War in films and most of them unanimously agreed that most Vietnam War films focuses on the American soldier, and that one of the major reasons that films about Vietnam War attracted the American audience. As the critic Susan Jeffords notes that 'Vietnam War narratives have noted, Vietnam War films function as a reflection and a revision of America's participation in the Vietnam War.' (Nishme, 2005, p. 259)

In conclusion, there is more than on way of depicting the enemy, the 'other'. Suid mentions how some filmmakers portrayed the enemy, for example, the Asians as barbarous enemy who machine-gunned fliers hanging in parachutes, whereas the Germans were portrayed as intellectuals possibly because their skin colour and cultural heritage aligned more closely to American society. (2002, p. 71) However, the Nazis in American films were depicted in one way as cultured people and intellectuals who sit around a conference table discussing cases, and in another way as brutes and sadists who enjoy killing others. The Vietnamese in American films, on the other hand were depicted as animals, uncultured people, uncivilised people who shoot to wound rather than kill, and barbarians who hide behind the trees in the jungles. Yet, there is a big huge difference in comparison between the two enemies 'Nazis and Vietnamese' who depicted in the American films.

In the following chapter I will discuss the representation of Iraqis and Arabs in Hollywood films in order to later examine how this compares with the representation of the Germans and Vietnamese discussed in this chapter.

Chapter Two

History of the Relationship between America and Iraq

> The war in Iraq, along with the occupation of that country by coalition forces pending the establishment of an Iraqi government, is the most significant event in the relationship with the countries of the Greater Middle East in the past half-century. (Rabasa, 2004, p. 52)

America has a long relationship with the Middle East and Iraq specifically. After WWII, America seized international control all over the world. Cal Jillson discusses the response of policymakers post-WWII, saying,

> American and allied policymakers responded [post-WWII] by building a set of international institutions that both embodied democratic and free market principles and guaranteed that the United States a leadership position within them. (2009, p. 439)

This suggests that the United States of America maintains strong international control. However, post-WWII the United States showed interest in the Middle East, as critics said, because of oil reserves. 'The Middle East in general has remained a centre of concern for the U.S. because of the West's dependency on the region's oil sources.' (Halabi, 2009)

In 1990, the ruler of Iraq, Saddam Hussein threatened to invade Kuwait. Some critics believed that this invasion would have caused oil prices to rise at an international level. In his book *The Gulf War of 1991*, Alastair Finlan states that 'by spring 1990, Saddam Hussein was desperately seeking a financial solution to his rapidly downward-spiralling economic and political situation.' (2009, p. 23) Consequently, the years of 1990 to 1991 witnessed the Iraqi invasion of Kuwait, followed by the U.S. military operations on the order of George Bush. Many writers and critics argued about the reason for the involvement of the U.S. military in the Gulf War, whether it was for the liberation of Kuwait, the oil reserves, or the promotion of democratisation (2009).

The First Gulf War ... triggered U.S. strategic interests within hours of the Iraqi invasion of Kuwait. The First Gulf War triggered an automatic response to defend Saudi Arabia and the smaller emirates from Iraqi invasion. The strategic interest was conflated with the economic interest in protecting the Gulf's oil supply. (Schwab, 2009)

Finlan argues about the cause of the involvement of U.S. troops as to liberate Kuwait and said that 'the naval commitment to the Gulf War was an important component of the overall strategy to liberate Kuwait' (2009). Moreover, Yaktub Halabi argues for the same case of U.S. involvement, saying,

The period after World War II saw an intensive and extensive expansion of US military and diplomatic involvement in the Middle East. The United States was historically disconnected from abuses of colonial policy in the area. (2009)

In the early 21st century, a decade after the First Gulf War ended, a series of four related suicide attacks were launched in the United States. The September 11 attacks were claimed to have been carried out by Al-Qaeda group leader, Osama bin Laden after he was portrayed to have claimed responsibility for the attacks in 2004. The United Sates reported that most of the hijackers who piloted the planes that attacked four buildings in New York, Pennsylvania and Washington D.C. were from Saudi Arabia. United States Administration claimed that the attacks were a conspiracy among radical Muslims against the United States, for which Osama bin Laden was the chief conspirator (Lelong, 2011).

The 9/11 terror attack were genuine disaster for the American people. This event would become a global catastrophe when the Bush-Cheney administration's "war on terror" mutated into a terror war that included an invasion of Afghanistan and Iraq. (Kellner, 2010, p. 101)

The response of the United States to the attacks was launching the "War on Terror." In October 2001, the United States started by invading Afghanistan, home of the Taliban, which was claimed to have been safe-harbouring Al-Qaeda for years (Fiscus, 2004). In 2003, the United States invaded Iraq as some U.S. officials accused the Iraqi President Saddam Hussein of supporting Al-Qaeda. According to Loretta Napoleoni, 'the Americans used such investigations to prove that there was a link between Saddam Hussein and al Qaeda.' (2003, p. 116) Yet, the invasion of Iraq led to an occupation of Iraq for years and the capture of Saddam Hussein by U.S. forces. In 2006, Saddam Hussein was hanged to death for committing crimes against humanity and other offenses. However, before the Iraq War, also known as the Second Gulf War, the governments of the United States of America and the United Kingdom claimed that Iraq owned weapons of mass destruction that created a threat to security (Nelson, 2004). However, in his book, *Petrodollar Warfare: Oil, Iraq and the Future of the Dollar,* William Crack reports the findings of his analysis of the Iraq War.

> Despite over 400 unfettered UN [United Nations] inspections before the 2003 invasion, and hundreds more after the war, there has been no reported evidence that Iraq had reconstituted any aspects of its previous WMD [weapons of mass destructions program]. (2005, p. 97)

Since then, other writers, critics and analysts in the Muslim world have said that the goal of launching the Iraq War was to cease control of the oil reserves, as Ron Geaves et al., states.

> The attack on Iraq has aroused deep suspicion in Muslims minds all over the world, even among the most moderate and liberal groups, that the agenda was about gaining a stronghold in the heart of the Middle East and about petroleum geopolitics. (2004)

The Representations of Iraqis in American War Films

The 'War on Terror' has continued to stir controversy since the 9/11 attacks until the capture of the most wanted man, Osama bin Laden in 2011. Since the 9/11 attacks, the enemy of the United Stated have been terrorists and Muslim extremists. More specifically, the boogiemen after 9/11 were Iraqis and Afghanis as their two countries were accused of harbouring Al-Qaeda. In this chapter I will examine how Iraqis have been portrayed in Hollywood since the 9/11 attacks. Specifically, this chapter will focus on the representation of Iraqis in films.

Hollywood films about Iraq and the Iraq War post 9/11 represent Iraqis in various ways. Analysis reveals that there are five ways of presenting the enemy as could be seen in the way of depicting of Iraqis in films. First, Iraqis in many movies are depicted as ignorant and uncivilised. For example, a movie based on the Iraq War, *The Hurt Locker* (2008), portrays the post invasion era in Iraq in 2004. It shows elite soldiers having put their lives at stake everyday for their country, the United States. William James, who is the leading role of the film played by Jeremy Renner, is a leader of the bomb squad in Bravo Company of a U.S. Army Explosive Ordnance Disposal (E.O.D.). James has unique skills and methods in destroying explosives, which baffle his two subordinate soldiers, Sergeant J.T. Sanborn played by Anthony Mackie, and Sergeant Owen Eldridge played by Brain Geraghty.

In some of its scenes, *The Hurt Locker* represents Iraqis as ignorant and uncivilised. These 'ignorant and uncivilised' Iraqis could be seen in scenes where American soldiers are driving their Humvee, telling Iraqis to get out of their way. This scene shows the chaos in which Iraqis live. They are portrayed as living in an uncivilised way: cars are driven chaotically, people speak to each other loudly, and people sitting on the sidewalk selling products who do not obey American soldiers when they order them to move.

Body of Lies (2008) is another film that shows the representation of Iraqis as ignorant and uncivilised. This film is based on a fictional novel written by David Ignatius. The film is starring Leonardo Dicaprio and Russell Crowe. The plot of the film is about an American spy, Roger Ferris played by Dicaprio, who is a CIA officer in the Middle East. He is on a mission to search for a fictional character, Jihadist and 'terrorist' called Al-Saleem, played by Alon Abutbul. Ed Hoffman is Ferris' supervisor who lives in Washington and authorises operations for Ferris by telephone. The film continues with the story in search of Al-Saleem. However, Al-Saleem is aware of the immanent raid so he escapes. To capture him, Ferris plans a fake suicide attack, but Al-Saleem is able to kidnap Ferris. Yet, by the end of the film, Al-Saleem was arrested and Ferris was saved by commandos.

In the scenes depicting Iraq, Iraqis are represented as uncivilised when Hoffman declares to his superior that the enemy they are searching for is 'unsophisticated', and it will be easy to capture them. The use of the word, 'unsophisticated' is synonymous with ignorance and lack of civility. Iraqis are dressed as beggars pleading for money at car windows revealing them as uncivilised.

Second, Iraqis are represented in Hollywood films as uneducated people. In *The Hurt Locker,* several scenes show how Iraqis are uneducated people who have nothing intelligent to say because they are illiterate. In the scene where the Americans are in the Humvee telling people to move away and no one responds simply because they do not understand the language. Another scene is the Iraqi boy who sells DVDs. This young boy sells porn DVDs with his uncle. This shows how much these Iraqis are uneducated where an underage child sells illegal DVDs.

Representation of uneducated Iraqis could also be seen in *Body of Lies*, as this film depicts Iraqis as Muslim extremists and terrorists who can blast any place in the world. The film shows the uneducated Iraqis who use the Holy Qur'an in the wrong way as they are trying to prove a point by interpreting verses in their interest. Moreover, the film shows traitors in Al-Qaeda who want to give up being extremists, and who do not want to take their own lives in the name of jihad.

> It should be noted, however, that a more balanced and sophisticated portrayal of Arabs and Muslims has been coming out of Hollywood studios... Such films as *Body of Lies* ... not only portray the complexities of the Middle East politics but also present a diversity of Arab and Muslim characters and their approaches to Islam. (Yasmeen, 2010, p. 152)

The depiction of Iraqis and Arabs in general as terrorists in *Body of Lies* is very clear. As many critics argue that the character of Al-Saleem is a surrogate of Osama bin Laden. Yet the most astonishing images of *Body of Lies* are accurate, as it has another step to locating Osama bin Laden with an aerial eyeball scan (Ebert, 2011). As Oliver Boyd-Barret et al., argue in the book *Hollywood and the CIA: Cinema, Defence and Subversion* that:

> The movie [*Body of Lies*] takes the treatment of Jihadist terrorism as part of the natural order of things, commiserates with it Western heroes, and

justifies its one-sided focus with on-screen representations of, and off-screen references to, fictional acts of terrorism in Sheffield, Manchester, and Amsterdam. (2011, p. 149)

Third, Hollywood films represent Iraqis as de-individuated. This representation of Iraqis could be seen in the movie *Green Zone* (2010) movie inspired by a non-fiction book *Imperial Life in the Emerald City* written by Rajiv Chandrasekaran. The book is about a documentary of life in the Green Zone in Baghdad, the capital city of Iraq. The film starts with General Mohammed Al-Rawi played by Yigal Naour, who is hiding in Baghdad on 13 March 2003. This General is waiting for American troops to invade Iraq, hoping to strike a deal with them so that he can get the troops on his side. The film then advances four weeks ahead and shows officer Roy Miller, played by Matt Damon, raiding a warehouse and searching for weapons of mass destruction. The story of the film continues on with the failure of finding any weapons of mass destruction, as Miller continuously receives false information. Miller tries to search the truth behind this falsified information to find out that the United States did not launch a war on Iraq because they suspect that Iraq owns weapons of mass destruction, but for the oil reserves that Iraq has.

Green Zone looks at an American war in a way almost no Hollywood movie ever has: We're [Americans] not the heroes, but the dupes. Its message is that Iraq's fabled "weapons of mass destruction" did not exist, and that neocons with the administration fabricated them, lied about them, and were ready to kill to cover up their deception. (Ebert, 2011, p. 224)

Green Zone represents Iraqis as de-individuated in the scenes between Miller and Freddy, played by Khalid Abdullah. Freddy 'represent[s] the everyday people of Baghdad who want an end to the violence and oppression in their country' (Caldwell, 2010). The reduction of self-awareness and loss of personal identity in Iraqi people in the film led to present them in one person who is part of a whole nation.

Fourth, the invisibility in the representation of Iraqis in Hollywood films could be seen in depicting Iraqis in a variety of films. Such films like *The Hurt Locker* and *Green Zone* represent Iraqis but those Iraqis are invisible in the film. As in *The Hurt Locker,* the film is all about the period post Iraq War and it is located in Iraq according to the story, but representation of Iraqis is invisible. The film focuses on the American soldiers and the problem that these soldiers faced during their mission in destroying the explosives. However, the film emphasises more on the sacrifices that the American soldiers make when they carry out their missions, and the loved ones they lose during rotations. As Stacey Peebles argues, '*The Hurt Locker* does a good job of articulating the challenges returning troops face when they are coming home and trying to assimilate back to normal life.' (2011, p. 173). *The Hurt Locker* ignores the main issue of the war and the conflict between the enemy and the Americans; instead it focuses on one side of the story.

> *The Hurt locker* has also been criticized for this lack of open engagement with the politics of the war…*The Hurt Locker* places its focus not on macro-political matters but on the details of soldier experiences. (Waksman, 2011, p. 195)

Green Zone focuses on the American soldiers as well. The invisibility of Iraqis could be noted as throughout the film the focus is on Miller as he is carrying out his mission in finding the weapons of mass destruction, the Green Zone, and the area that is occupied by the American military. The reduced emphasis on Iraqis is shown in this film. However, the war in the *Green Zone* could be more between the Pentagon and CIA, rather than between the U.S. and Iraq, whereas the film is supposedly about the Iraq War after the invasion.

> *Green Zone* will no doubt be under fire from those who are still defending the fabricated intelligence we [Americans] used as an excuse to invade Iraq. Yet, the film is fiction, employs far-fetched coincidences, and improbably places one man at the center of all the action. (Ebert, 2011, p. 225)

The fifth and last way of representing Iraqis in films is depicting Iraqis as apathetic people, those who are doing nothing and surrendering to the inevitable. Representing the apathetic Iraqis could be seen clearly in *The Hurt Locker*. The movie shows Iraqis as people who look through the windows to the American soldiers; these Iraqis are just staring at them without doing anything. Another scene that shows the apathetic Iraqis who are surrendering to the inevitable is when James goes to the centre of Baghdad to search for the family of the young boy who sells DVDs. Most of the Iraqis who are presented are sitting in coffee shops playing cards, or sitting on the sidewalk dealing with each other or with their products, as if nothing happened in their country.

In this chapter I have discussed how Iraqis and Arabs are represented in Hollywood war films. Although they are often invisible in this films, when they are seen, they are generally de-individuated and portrayed as uncivilised, uneducated and apathetic. In the following chapter I will compare this with the representation of the Nazis and Vietnamese.

Chapter Three

Depicting the Enemy

> What is an Arab? In countless films, Hollywood alleges the answer: Arabs are brute murderers, sleazy rapists, religious fanatics, oil-rich dimwits and abusers of women. (Shaheen, 2009)

Arabs, including Iraqis, are depicted in Hollywood films in particular ways, usually as primitive and uncivilised brutes. In her book *The Depiction of Terrorists in Blockbuster Hollywood, 1980-2001: An Analytical Study*, Helena Vanhala discusses the way that Arabs are stereotyped in Hollywood films. She points out that '[o]ne of the most vilified and stereotyped groups in Hollywood is Arabs' and 'Hollywood portrayal of Arabs has been distorted, and the industry has been dehumanizing Arabs' (2011). The similarities in the depiction of the "enemy" in the case of Arabs and Nazis lies in the fact that both of them are represented as brutes. Whereas Nazis tend to be represented as intellectuals, most of the representations of Arabs in Hollywood films depict them as primitive, according to Vanhala.

In *Body of Lies*, the brutish depiction of Arabs can be seen in the scene where the Jihadists led by Al-Saleem capture Ferris and torture him brutally and mercilessly by using a variety of sharp weapons. A similar scene in *The Great Escape* is when Squadron Leader Roger Bartlett is captured and executed by Gestapo officers.

While many scenes in Hollywood films show Arabs as brutes, the representation of Arabs as intellectuals is rare. However, sometimes Arabs are depicted as intellectuals in a similar way to the Nazis. The character of Hani Salam in *Body of Lies* is depicted as an intellectual westernised Arab who has skills and power. When Ferris goes to Jordan to find Al-Saleem, he meets the head of the Jordanian General Intelligence Department Hani Salaam, played by Mark strong. Salaam plays the typical westernised Arab character. He always wears a suit, he looks like a western man who lives a luxurious life including expensive cars. The story proceeds to Salaam warning Ferris not to lie to him, but

Ferris does. Salaam exiles Ferris from Jordan after he tortures Ferris. By the end, the viewer finds out that Salaam uses the CIA officer Ferris to capture the terrorist Al-Saleem.

The intellectual and brutish character of Salaam is similar to the character of Colonel Paul Kramer, the Gestapo officer in *Where Eagles Dare*. When the Germans capture Carnaby, Kramer carries out an interrogation. In the interrogation scene, Colonel Karmer is portrayed as an intellectual. He wears a smart uniform and drinks while carrying out the interrogation in a conference room that is furnished with luxurious furniture. These scenes are examples of how Arabs and Nazis are depicted in Hollywood films as brutes as well as intellectuals.

There are many similarities between the representation of Vietnamese and Arabs in Hollywood films. As mentioned earlier, the dominant character in depicting Vietnamese in Hollywood films is portraying them as primitive, uncivilised and savages. Furthermore, in some films Vietnamese are invisible and rarely seen. This manner of representing Vietnamese could be seen in many Iraq War films that depict Iraqis.

Produced in two different decades, two films have similar scenes although one film is about the Vietnam War and portraying the Vietnamese and the other is about the Iraq War and portraying the Iraqi Arabs. *The Deer hunter*, produced in 1987, and *Body of Lies*, produced in 2008, have similar scenes that portray the Vietnamese and the Iraqis savages. In *Body of Lies*, the scene where the Jihadists capture Omar Sadiki played by Ali Suliman, is similar to the Russian Roulette scene where the Vietnamese capture the three friends. The Jihadists in *Body of Lies* capture Sadiki and interrogate him about whether or not he planned a terrorist attack. When he admits his innocence and does not set up the attack, they torture him savagely and kill him. They then throw his body in the desert. A similar scene is in *The Deer Hunter*, when the savage Northern Vietnamese ask the Southern Vietnamese man to kill the Americans, he refuses because he can not do it. They force him to shoot himself, and they then throw his body in the sea. In these two scenes both Arabs and Vietnamese are portrayed as savages and merciless people.

There are many other scenes in Vietnam War films and Iraq War films that depict the primitive and uncivilised Vietnamese and Iraqis. The two themes of dehumanising the enemy and the invisible enemy are evident in these kinds of films. In *The Hurt Locker* and *Body of Lies*, these two themes are seen in the representation of Iraqis where in both films, the enemy is dehumanised and/or is invisible. The dehumanisation of the enemy in *The Hurt Locker* is illustrated by portraying barbarian Iraqis who speak loudly across the street and who ride in cars in a disorganised and chaotic manner. The theme of dehumanising the enemy again could be seen in *Body of Lies* where the film shows Iraqis as uncivilised and uneducated people in many scenes. In the film scenes located in Iraq, Iraqis are portrayed as uncivilised and primitive people, who live in the desert and have no electricity. In comparison to Vietnamese, similar scenes could be seen in *Platoon*, in which the Vietnamese are represented as people who live in jungles among snakes and insects, and wear red headbands.

The second theme where the Iraqi enemy is invisible is evident in *The Hurt Locker.* In this film, all Iraqis are represented as one person, who is less visible despite the fact that the film is about the Iraq War, and not only about the sacrifices of the American soldiers. This is exactly the same as in Vietnam War films such as *Apocalypse Now* where the film is about Vietnam War, yet most of the movie is about the story of the American soldier who suffers from war, at the same time neglecting the presence of the Vietnamese.

There are clear similarities between the depictions of the enemy in Hollywood films. Among Nazis and Iraqis, both are represented as intellectuals, and among Vietnamese and Iraqis, both are represented as primitive, uncivilised savages.

Always an Enemy

> [The United States has] been surprised this past century by the rise of
> communism, the rise of Nazism, and the rise of Islamic
> fundamentalism...Muslim fundamentalism is fast becoming the chief
> threat to global [and United States] peace and security...It is akin to the
> menace posted by Nazism and fascism in the 1930s and then by
> communism in the 50s. (Qureshi and Sells, 2003)

Fawaz A. Gerges analyses the enemy of the United States in his book,
America and Political Islam: Clash of Cultures or Clash of Interests? He notes
that Islam is the alternative enemy of the United States after the fall of Nazism
post WWII, and the death of Communism after the collapse of the Soviet Union
(1999). Since WWII, America has always had an enemy. The Nazi regime was
primarily the first enemy of the United States and the world in general. The Nazi
party was founded in the 1920s and it gained power until it dissolved by the end
of WWII in 1945. At that time, according to Thomas Noble et al. 'the Nazi regime
enjoyed considerable popular support' (2011). Moreover, Christian Leits
examines Nazism and the Nazi policy in his book *Nazi Foreign Policy, 1933-
1941: the Road to Global War*. He states that 'no doubt that Nazi Germany's
policy towards South-eastern Europe was of pivotal importance to the rest of
Europe, indeed the world' (2004, p. 93).

Regarding the power enjoyed by the Nazi party, there was a unique
position led by the United States among all powers involved in the Second World
War (Farrell, 2004). Joseph Farrell discusses the fear of Nazism by the United
States, writing that 'for the last time in [United States] history [during WWII], it
was able to undertake military operations on a global scale relatively free of the
fear of enemy reprisal.' (2004, p. 89) After Pearl Harbour and the victory of the
United States in WWII, Hollywood films created and constructed a way of
presenting the enemy, where the Nazis Germans are portrayed as the enemy.
McLaughlin and Parry examine the way Hollywood constructs the enemy, noting
that 'one frequently heard truism is that Hollywood films crudely and obviously
present the enemy [Nazis] as Other to the point of denying their humanity'
(2006). At this point, Hollywood films that dealt with Nazis as enemies were
commonly and usually a mixture of warnings against this regime (Schindler,

1979). Nazis were the enemy that Hollywood films presented until the rise of communism, the second enemy to the United States after the fall of Nazism.

> The enemy image of communism was a powerful cognitive force in the making of U.S. foreign policy following World War II and continues to have a powerful legacy, even as the United States enters the twenty-first century. (Rosati and Scott, 2011, p. 281)

The rise and power of communism post WWII threatened many countries all over the world making communism the second enemy facing the United States. Consequently, the fear that communism was increasingly spreading caused the United States and the Western world to launch a war against communism led by the Soviet Union in what is known as the Cold War. For approximately six decades, the Cold War continued causing political and military tension between the two camps, the United States and Western world against the Soviet Union and other communist countries. At that time, the main enemy according to the United States was communism, where Hollywood took the Vietnam War and Vietnamese as a symbol of the communist enemy. William M. Arkin makes the argument that Hollywood and its filmmakers represent the Vietnam War as symbolic of the communist villains. He notes that a whole series of movies about the Vietnam War such as *The Deer Hunter, Platoon, Apocalypse Now, The Green Berets* (1986), and the series of *Rambo* movies become symbolic of notification to the risk of the spreading of communism (Ackland, 1986).

In 1991, the fear of communism vanished after the dissolution of the Soviet Union and the fall of communism. With the fall of communism, the new enemy of the United States appears. In 1990, one year before the fall of communism and the launching of the Gulf War between the United States and Iraq, Islam became the main opponent to the United States which was later heightened by the 9/11 attacks. The typical "bad guys" shifted from Communists to Arabs directly after the collapse of the Soviet Union (Pennington, 2009). Yet, the 'War on Terror' begins and 'for a full century before September 11, 2002, America's boogeyman was the Arab' (Shora, 2009). In his book, *Islam and Jihad: Prejudice Versus Reality,* Abdul Gafoor Noorani states that 'to some Americans, searching for a new enemy against whom to test our mettle and power, after the death of communism, Islam is the preferred antagonist' (2002, p. 162). Since the

Gulf War, Hollywood films often represent Muslims as the enemy. Specifically, after the invasion and occupation of Iraq in 2004, Hollywood films take Iraq War as a symbol to portray the concept of war against Islam generally, not only Iraqis. Moreover, Hollywood representation of Muslims in most Iraq War films depicts Muslims as the "bad guys" who might ruin the world. Jack M. Shaheen describes the way Hollywood portrays Arabs in films by examining over 900 films produced by Hollywood in his book *Reel Bad Arabs: How Hollywood Vilifies a People*. Shaheen states that 'Hollywood portrays Arabs as the systematic, pervasive and unapologetic degradation and dehumanization of a people.' (2009)

In more than three decades, Hollywood uses its films to portray three enemies, Nazis, Communists, and Arabs. According to William Blum, America needs an enemy for a purpose or mission. He argues that the 'U.S. actually needs enemies to justify budgets and protect jobs' (2008). Throughout a long history of the United States, the economy of the entire nation has been served by an overseas policy (2008). In their book, *The Merchants of Fear: Why they Want us to be Afraid,* Christopher Catherwood and Joe Divanna examine the reasons why the United States needs an enemy at all times. They state that 'fear has always been a ready tool of [the United States] government to manipulate public opinion in the same way that business uses fear to sell products.' (2008)

Accordingly, there are two possible reasons for the need for an enemy by the United States. First, an enemy keeps the country's economy healthy; as an example, the economy of the United States improved after WWII. American economist R.A. Easterlin researched the American economy post WWII where his studies led him to conclude that "the economic factor accounts to a great extend for the postwar 'baby boom' in the United States" (1975). Regarding the Arabs, the author Mohammed El- Bendary states that:

> Most Arabs believe that as long as America is powerful militarily and remains the world's single superpower, it will continue its invasions of other nations in order to gain financially and protect its markets worldwide, which are the soul of its capitalist system. (2011, p. 136)

The second reason is to keep the people under fear and oppression. Byron Ben Renz examines how the enemy is needed by the United States to keep people afraid, stating that:

> The creation of fear needs to be associated with an enemy, and an enemy can be defined most concretely by creating a dichotomous image…a government [United States] uses the idea of common enemy as a method of social control, a method of reinforcing the political, economic and cultural values of the nation. (2010, p. 56).

Shaheen makes an argument about the way Arabs are represented in Hollywood productions, noting that Hollywood is a great national entertainer, and the most effective teacher of young. Indeed, 'Hollywood is the leading source of propagandistic images that damage and isolate some citizens' (2009). According to Hollywood, the boogeyman during WWII was the Nazis. When the Nazis retired, the alternative became the communists. The fall of communism led the way for Islam and Arabs to be the boogeyman of Hollywood films. Since 9/11 attacks, Arabs have been portrayed increasingly worse in movies such as Iraq War films.

The Choice of Arabs

The Second Gulf War, also known as the Iraq War, gave Hollywood a chance to represent Iraqi Arabs in war films. The representation of Arabs and Muslims, as many critics and writers argue, is that of uncivilised brutes. After the occupation of Iraq, some films such as *Body of Lies* portray Arabs as intellectuals as in the character of Hani Salam. The choice in representing Iraqis or Arabs and Muslims in Hollywood Iraq War films stays mostly the same. Although Hollywood represents Arabs as westernised, civilised and intellectuals at the same time they are the brutish Arabs who are represented in war films before the Second Gulf War or Iraq War. In some Iraq War films after the actual invasion and occupation of Iraq, Arabs and Muslims are represented as people who have been influenced by the American occupation and who are becoming more civilised by this occupation. For example, in *Body of Lies*, when Ferris accepts the nurse's invitation to visit her at home, he meets her nephews, two young boys between seven to nine years old. Ferris asks them whether or not they like their mother's cooking. The young boys tell Ferris that they do not like their mother's cooking as they prefer hamburgers. This scene shows how the Iraqi people are becoming westernised, having been affected by the American culture.

Hollywood's representation of Arabs and Muslims appears to offer a choice. On one hand, Muslims and Arabs are sometimes represented as invisible people where they are lost in the story and are rarely seen in a speaking role such as in *The Hurt Locker*. On the other hand, Arabs have also been represented as savages and an unsophisticated enemy as the Vietnamese have been. This manner of portraying Arabs could be seen very often in many Hollywood films about Iraq War such as *Body of Lies*. Alternatively, some Hollywood films represent Arabs as intellectuals, and perhaps even brutes, as were Nazis who were a worthy enemy. Hani Salaam's character in *Body of Lies* is an illustrative example. Furthermore, the dominant character of portraying Muslims and Arabs in Hollywood films is depicting them as brutal, uncivilised savages as Shaheen notes.

> Seen through Hollywood's distorted lenses, Arabs look different and threatening. Projected along racial and religious lines, the stereotypes are deeply ingrained in American cinema. From 1896 until today, filmmakers have collectively indicated all Arabs as Public enemy #1—brutal, heartless, uncivilized religious fanatics and money-mad cultural "others" bent on terrorizing civilized Westerners. (2009)

The portrayal of the enemy "other", the Nazis, Vietnamese and Arabs in Hollywood films has a common representation, which is the character of the villain. The portrayal of Muslims and Arabs in Hollywood films post 9/11 is connected with terrorism, where dozens of films produced after 9/11 attacks typically depict Muslims and Arabs as terrorist villains (Vanhala, 2011). Nazis as well are portrayed as villains in Hollywood films being identified in the public mind with the Nazis villains (Elsaesser, 2000). Hollywood films about Vietnam War also represent the Vietnamese as menacing and unscrupulous villains (Tator et al., 1998).

Conclusion

Hollywood representations of Arabs and Muslims have been deep-rooted in the Western conceptualisation ever since the first contacts with Arabs and Muslims (Ridouani, 2011). Before the 9/11 attacks, the portrayal of Arabs and Muslims in Hollywood films is well known and recognised in the West as ignorant, primitive, uncivilised wealthy people with slaves. However, after the 9/11 attacks the depiction of Arabs and Muslims did not change much, as the portrayed characters became increasingly connected with the terms terrorists, brutes, savages, extremists and fundamentalists. Mostly, the same stereotypes of Arabs and Muslims are promoted by Hollywood, as Shaheen noted (2009). In addition, Hollywood preserves a continuum of representing Muslims and Arabs as the "other," and even the "enemy".

In his book *Orientalism*, Edward Said uses and redefines the term Orientalism to a collection of wrong and false assumptions motivating Western attitudes and approaches toward the Middle East (Said, 1994). Said examines the way the West sees Muslims and Arabs. Said notes that Muslims and Arabs have been misrepresented in Western media. Furthermore, Robert S. Fortner and P. Mark Fackler examine the portrayal of Arabs and Muslims in Western Media in their book, *The Handbook of Global Communication and Media Ethics*. They note that 'as early as the first years of the twentieth century, Arabs were portrayed as exotic Bedouins [primitive], with harems [women], sheiks [wealthy old men], and belly dancers' (2011).

In another book by Shaheen, *Guilty: Hollywood's Verdict on Arabs After 9/11*, he analyses the way Hollywood has been stereotyping Arabs. He also shows how Arabs were used as shorthand for the "enemy" and the "other". Shaheen adds and writes that almost all of Hollywood's post 9/11 attacks films legitimise a depiction of Arabs as stereotyped villain-sheikhs and terrorists (2008). In Hollywood films after 9/11, the focus mostly is on portraying Iraq as the main region of the Middle East. In *Body of Lies*, the film starts in Iraq; in *The Hurt Locker*, the mission of the bomb disposal soldiers takes place in Iraq during the war; and in *Green Zone*, the squad investigator takes his duty in Iraq after four weeks from the invasion. Many films after 9/11 have at least a brief about Iraq as part of the story. This shows that in Hollywood, Iraq may be considered a symbol for the entire Arab or Muslim world.

> Hollywood's motion pictures reach nearly everyone. Cinematic illusions are created, nurtured, and distributed worldwide, reaching viewers in more than 100 countries, from Iceland to Thailand. Arab images have an effect not only on international audiences, but on international moviemakers as well. (2009)

In conclusion, Arabs and Muslims in Hollywood films are portrayed in a specific way. This portrayal did not vary across the time period before the 9/11 attacks or after. However, the portrayal of Arabs and Muslims became worse in Hollywood films. Some films portray Arabs as intellectuals, yet they remain villains. The misrepresentation of Arabs in Hollywood films could be seen very clearly in hundreds of films, not only in films about the Iraq War. For centuries, Hollywood films may be seen by millions of people. Yet, Hollywood has not been fair or has done justice in the representation of Arabs and Muslims, especially Iraqis.

LIST OF REFERENCES

Articles

- Shaheen, Jack G. (1997) 'Arab and Muslim Stereotyping in American Pupular Culture.' In Edmund A. Walsh (ed.) *Center for Muslim-Christian Understanding: History and International Affairs.* Washington D.C., 1-80.

Books

- Birdwell, Michael E. (1999) *Celluloid Soldiers: The Warner Bros.'s. Campaign Against Nazism.* New York and London: New York University Press.

- Biskupski, Mieczyslaw B. (2010) *Hollywood's War With Poland, 1939-1945.* Lexington, Kentucky: The University Press of Kentucky.

- Booker, Keith M. (2007) *From Box to Ballot Box: The American Political Film.* Westport, CT: Praeger Publisher.

- Boyd-Barrett, Oliver, Herrera, David and Baumann, Jim (2011) *Hollywood and the CIA: Cinema, Defense and Subversion.* New York: Routledge.

- Briley, Ron (2001*) The Sun Comes Out Tomorrow.* In Young, Nancy Beck, Willian D. Pederson and Byron W. Daynes, eds (2001) *Franklin D. Roosevelt and The Shaping of American Political Culture.* Armonk, New York: M. E. Sharpe.

- Browne, Pat and Ray Browne, eds (2001) *The Guide to United States Popular Culture.* Madison, Wisconsin: The University of Wisconsin Press.

- Brunsch, Claudia (2005) *Stereotyping as a Phenomenon in intercultural Communication.* Norderstedt Germany: Grin Verlag.

- Carre, J.J., P. Dubois and E. Malinvaud (1975) *French Economic Growth.* John P. Hatfield (trans.) Stanford, California: Oxford University Press.

- Catherwood, Christopher and Joseph Divanna (2006) *Merchants of Fear: Why They Want us to be Afraid.* Guilford, CT: The Globe Pequote Press.

- Clark, William R. (2005) *Petrodollar Warfare: Oil, Iraq and the future of the Dollar.* Canada: New Society Publisher.

- Douglas, Kellner (2010) *Cinema Wars: Hollywood Film and Politics in the Bush-Cheney Era.* United Kingdom: Wiley-Blackwell.

- Duiker, William J. and Jackson J. Spielvogel (2011) *The Essential World History, Volume two: since 1500.* Boston, MA: Wadsworth.

- Ebert, Roger (2011) *Roger Ebert's Movie Yearbook 2011.* Kansas City, Missouri: Andrews McMeel Publishing, LLC.

- El-Bendary, Mohamed (2011) *The "Ugly American" in the Arab Mind: Why Do Arabs Resent America?.* Washington, D.C.: Potomac Books Inc.

- Eloranta, Jari (2002) *War and Film.* In Stanley Sandler, ed. (2002) *Ground Warfare: An International Encyclopedia Volume 1.* Santa Barbara, CA: ABC-CLIO, Inc. Publisher.

- Elsaesser, Thomas (2000) *Weimar Cinema and After: Germany's Historical Imaginary.* United States and Canada: Routledge.

- Farrell, Joseph (2004) *Reich of the Black Sun: Nazi Secret Weapons & The Cold War Allied Legend.* Kempton, Illinois: Adventures Unlimited Press.

- Fiscus, James W. (2004) *America's War in Afghanistan.* New York: The Rosen Publishing Group, Inc.

- Fortner, Robert and Mark Fackler (2011) *The Handbook of Global Communication and Media Ethics.* United States: Wiley Blackwell.

- Geaves, Gabriel, Haddad and Smith, eds (2004) *Islam and the West Post 9/11.* England: Ashgate Publishing Company.

- Gerges, Fawaz (1999) *America and Political Islam: Clash of Cultures or Clash of Interests?.* New York: Cambridge University Press.

- Gershoni, Israel and James Jankowski (2010) *Confronting Fascism in Egypt: Dictatorship Versus Democracy in the 1930s.* Stanford, CA: Stanford University Press.

- Gianos, Phillip L. (1998) *Politics and Politicians in American Film.* Westport, CT: Praeger Publisher.

- Gilly, Thomas, Yakov Gilinskiy and Vladimir A. Sergevnin, eds (2009) *The Ethics of Terrorism: Innovative Approaches from an International Perspectives.* Springfield, Illinois: Charles C Thomas-Publisher, Ltd.

- Goonetilleke, D.C.R.A. (2007) *Joseph Conrad's Heart of Darkness.* Abingdon, Oxon OX: Routledge.

- Halabi, Yakub (2009) *U.S. Foreign Policy in the Middle East: from Crisis to Change.* England: Ashgate Publishing Limited.

- Hamilton, John (2012) *World War II: the Final Years. United States*: ABDO Publishing Company.

- Hansen, Valerie and Kenneth R. Curtis (2010) *Voyages in World History*. Boston, MA: Wadsworth.

- Ian, Roberts (2010) *Tinker, Tailor, Nazi, Sailor: Stereotypes of German Combatants in Wolfgang Petersen's Das Boot*. In Brigid Hianes, Stephen Parker and Colin Riordan, eds (2010) *Aesthetics and Politics in Modern German Culture*. Bern, Switzerland: Peret Lang AG, International Academic Publishers.

- Jackson, Ashley (2006) *The British Empire and the Second World War.* United Kingdom: MPG Books Ltd.

- Jillson, Cal (2009) *American Government: Political Development and Institutional Change*. New York: Routledge.

- Kamalipour, Yahya R. ed (1995) *The U.S. Media and the Middle East: Image and Perception.* Westport, CT: Praeger Publisher.

- Kamin, Dan (2008) *The Comedy of Charlie Chap;in: Artistry in Motion.* Lanham, Maryland: Scarecrow Press.

- Keith, Booker M. (1999) *Film and The American Left: A Research Guide.* Westport, Ct: Greenwood Press.

- Koppes, Clayton and Black, Gregory D. (1987) *Hollywood Goes to War: How Politics, Profits, and Propaganda Shaped World War II Movies.* United States: The Free Press.

- Laqueur, Walter and Judith Baumel (2001) The Holocaust Encyclopaedia. United States: Walter Laqueur.

- Leitz, Christian (2004) *Nazi Foreign policy, 1933-1941: the Road to Global War.* New York: Routledge.

- Lelong, M.P. (2011) *9/11 Deceptions.* Bloomington, IN: Xlibris Publisher.

- Luther, Catherine A., Carolyn Ringer Lepre and Naeemah Clark (2011) *Diversity in U.S. Mass Media.* West Sussex, U.K.: Wiley-Blackwell.

- Mackie, Diane, David Hamilton, Joshua Susskind and Francine Rosselli (1996) *Social Psychological Foundations of Stereotype Formation.* In Macrae, Neil C., Charles Stangor and Miles Hewstone, eds (1996) *Stereotypes and Stereotyping.* New York, NY: A Division of Guilford Publication.

- Manchel, Frank (1990) *Film Study: An Analytical Bibliography, Volume 1.* Salem, Massachusetts: Associated University Presses.

- Mclaughlin, Robert and Sally E. Parry (2006) *We'll Always Have the Movies: American Cinema During World War II.* Lexington, Kentucky: The University Press of Kentucky.

- Napoleoni, Loretta (2003) *Insurgent Iraq: AlZarqawi and The New Generation.* New York: Seven Stories Press.

- Nishme, Leilani (2005) *Remembering Vietnam in the 1980s, White Skin, White Masks: Vietnam War Films and Radicalized Gaze.* In David Holloway and John Beck, eds (2005) *American Visual Cultures.* New York: Oxford International Publishers.

- Noble, Thomas F. X., Barry Strauss, Duane J. Osheim, Kristen B. Neuschel, Elinor A. Accampo, David D. Robert and et al. (2009) *Western Civilization: Beyond Boundaries, Since 1560.* Boston, MA: Wadsworth.

- Noorani, Abdul Gafoor (2002) *Islam & Jihad: Prejudice Versus Reality.* New York: Zed Books Ltd.

- Palmer, William J. (1993) *The Films of the Eighties.* United States: The Board of Trustees.

- Peebles, Stacy (2011) *Welcome to the Suck: Narrating the American Soldier's Experience in Iraq.* London: Cornell University Press.

- Pennington, Brian K. (ed) (2012) *Teaching Religion and Violence.* New York: Oxford University Press.

- Quart, Leonardo and Albert Auster (2011) *American Film and Society Since 1945.* Santa Barbara, CA: Praeger Publisher.

- Qureshi, Emran and Michael A. Sells (eds) (2003) *The News Crusaders: Constructing the Muslim Enemy.* New York: Columbia University Press.

- Rabasa, Angel (2004) *The Muslim World After 9/11.* Santa Monica, CA: Rand Corporation.

- Renz, Byron Ben (2010) *Our Own Worst Enemy as Protector of Ouerselves: Stereotypes, Schema and Typifications as Integral Elements in the Persuasive Process.* Lanham, Maryland: University Press of America.

- Ridouani, Driss (2011) The Representation of Arabs and Muslims in Western Media. Meknes: 1-15.

- Rosati, Jerel and James M. Scott (2010) *The Politics of United States Foreign Policy.* Boston, MA: Wadsworth.

- Ross, Steve (2004) *Confession of a Nazi Spy: Warner Brothers, Anti-Fascism, and the Politicization of Hollywood,* In *Warner's' War: Politics Pop Culture & Propaganda in Wartime Hollywood.* pp. 48-59. Los Angeles, CA: Norman Lear Center Press.

- Rubin, Steve Jay (2011) *Combat Films: American Realism, 1945-2010.* Jefferson, North Carolina: Mcfarland & Company Inc. Publishers.

- Ryan, Maureen (2008) *The Other Side of Grief: The Home Front and the Aftermath in American Narratives of the Vietnam War.* Massachusetts, U.S.: University of Massachusetts Press.

- Said, Edward (1994) Orientalism. New York: Random House, Inc.

- Schwab, Orrin (2009) *The Gulf Wars and the United States: Shaping the Twenty First Century.* Westport, CT: Praeger Publisher.

- Shirer, William (1991) *The Rise and Fall of the Third Reich.* London: The Random House Group Ltd.

- Shaheen, Jack G. (2009) *Reel Bad Arabs: How Hollywood Verifies a People.* Northampton, Massachusetts: Olive Branch Press.

- Shaheen, Jack G. (2008) *Guilty: Hollywood's Verdict on Arabs After 9/11.* Northampton, Massachusetts: Olive Branch Press.

- Shora, Nawar (2009) *The Arab-American Handbook: A guide to the Arab, Arab-American & Muslim Worlds.* Seattle, WA: Cune Press.

- Solheim, Bruce O. (2006) *A Vietnam War Era: A personal Journey.* Westport, CT: Praeger Publisher.

- Suid, Lawrence H. (2002) Guts and Glory: *The Making of the American Military Image in Film.* Lexington, Kentucky: The University Press of Kentucky.

- Tator Carol, Frances Henry and Winston Mattis (1998) *Challenging Racism in the Arts: Case Studies of the Controversy and Conflict.* London: University of Toronto Press Incorporated.

- Thomas, Christopher (2009) *Friend, Foe and Friend: The German Image in America World War II Films*. In Jonathan C. Friedman, ed (2009) *Performing Difference: Representations of "The Other" in Film and Theater*. Lanham, Maryland: University Press of America.

- Vanhala, Helena (2011) *The Depiction of Terrorists in Blockbuster Hollywood films, 1980-2001: An Analytical Study*. Jefferson, North Carolina: McFarland & Company, Inc., Publishers.

- Vandermey, Randall, Verne Meyer, John Rys and Pat Sebranek (2009) *The College Writer: A Guide to Thinking, Writing and Researching with the 2009 MLA Update*. Boston, MA: Wadsworth.

- Waksman, Steve (2011) *The War on Terror*. In Fisher, Joseph P. and Flota, Brain, eds (2011) *The Politics of Post 9/11 Music, Trauma, and the Music Industry in the time of Terror*. England: Ashgate Publishing Company.

- Watson, James (1998) *Media Communication: An Introduction to Theory and Process*. New York: Palgrave.

- Weber, Jurgen (2004) Germany 1945-1990. Nicholas T. Parsons (trans) Budapest, Hungary: Central European University Share.

- Woodman, Brain J. (2005) *Represented in the Margins: Images of African American Soldiers in Vietnam War Combat Films*. In Robert T. Eberwein, ed (2005) *The War Film*. United States: Rutgers.

Films

- *Apocalypse Now* (1979) [DVD] dir. Francis Ford Coppola, prod. Francis Ford Coppola.

- *Body of Lies* (2008) [DVD] dir. Ridley Scott, prod. Sir Ridley Scott and Donald De Line.

- *Confessions of a Nazi Spy* (2010 edition) (1939) [DVD] dir. Anatole Litvak, prod. Hal B. Wallis, Jack L. Warner and Robert Lord.

- *Green Zone* (2010) [DVD] dir. Paul Greengrass, prod. Tim Bevan, Eric Fellner, Lloyd Levin and Paul Greengrass.

- *Platoon* (1986) [DVD] dir. Oliver Stone, prod. Arnold Kopelson.

- Rambo (2008) [DVD] dir. Sylvester Stallone, prod. Kevin King, Avil Lerner and John Thompson.

- *Rambo III* (1988) DVD] dir. Peter Mcdonald, prod. Buzz Feitshans, Mario Kassan and Amrew G. Vajna.

- *Rambo: First Blood* (1982) [DVD] dir. Ted Kotcheff, prod. Buzz Feitshans, Mario Kassar and Andrew G. Vajna.

- *Rambo: First Blood II* (1985) [DVD] dir. George P. Cosmatos, prod. Buzz Feitshans.

- *The Deer Hunter* (1978) [DVD] dir. Michael Cimino, prod. Barry Spikings, Michael Deeley, Michael Cimino and John Peverall.

- *The Dirty Dozen* (special edition) (1967) [DVD] dir. Robert Aldirch, prod. Kenneth Hyman.

- *The Great Dictator* (two disc special edition) (1940) [DVD] dir. Charlie Chaplin and Wheeler Dryden, prod. Charlie Chaplin.

- *The Great Escape* (definitive edition) (1963) [DVD] dir. John Sturges, prod. John Sturges.

- *The Green Berets* (1968) [DVD] dir. John Wayne, Ray Kellogg and Leroy, prod. Michael Wayne.

- *The Hurt Locker* (2008) [DVD] dir. Kathryn Bigelow, prod. Kathryn Bigelow, Mark Boal, Nicholas Chartier and Greg Shapiro.

- *Where Eagles Dare* (1968) [DVD] dir. Brian G. Hutton, prod. Elliott Lastner and Jerry Gershwin.

Journals

- Ackland, len (1986) 'Bulletin of the Atomic Sientists: Soviet Party Congress, Star Wars Threatens Satellites U.S. Strategic Intelligence.' *A Magazine of Science and World Affairs*. 3 (8), pp. 6-8.

- Blum, William (2006) *Rouge State: A Guide to the world's Only Superpower*. United Kingdom: Zed Books Ltd.

- Shaheen, Jack G. (1986) 'Media Coverage of the Middle East: Perception and Foreign Policy.' *The Annals of the American Academy of Political and Social Science*. 482 (1), pp. 160-175.

- El-Farra, Nermeen (1996) 'Arabs and the Media.' *Journal of Media Psychology*. 1 (2), http://www.naba.org.uk/CONTENT/articles/Diaspora/Arabs_&_Media_Fa rra.htm (accessed 10 May 2012)

- Shaheen, Jack G. (2000) 'Hollywood's Muslim Arabs.' *The Muslim World*. 90 (1-2), pp. 22-42.

Websites:

1. Caldwell, Thomas (2010) *Film review – Green Zone (2010).* http://www.rrr.org.au/whats-going-on/reviews/green-zone-2010/ (accessed 12 April 2011)

2. McConnell, Marla (2003) *Media and Gender Stereotyping.* http://serendip.brynmawr.edu/local/scisoc/sports03/papers/mmcconnell.html (accessed 4 March 2012)

3. Nelson, Bill (2004) *Congressional Record: New Information on Iraq's Possession of Weapons of Mass Destruction.* http://www.fas.org/irp/congress/2004_cr/s012804b.html (accessed 22 April 2011).

I want morebooks!

Buy your books fast and straightforward online - at one of world's fastest growing online book stores! Environmentally sound due to Print-on-Demand technologies.

Buy your books online at
www.morebooks.shop

Kaufen Sie Ihre Bücher schnell und unkompliziert online – auf einer der am schnellsten wachsenden Buchhandelsplattformen weltweit! Dank Print-On-Demand umwelt- und ressourcenschonend produziert.

Bücher schneller online kaufen
www.morebooks.shop

KS OmniScriptum Publishing
Brivibas gatve 197
LV-1039 Riga, Latvia
Telefax: +371 686 204 55

info@omniscriptum.com
www.omniscriptum.com

Printed by Books on Demand GmbH, Norderstedt / Germany